The INSIDE GUIDE

EARLY AMERICAN HISTORY

The Story of Immigration and Migration

By Bert Wilberforce

Cavendish Square

Published in 2024 by Cavendish Square Publishing, LLC
2544 Clinton Street Buffalo, NY 14224

Website: cavendishsq.com

Library of Congress Cataloging-in-Publication Data

Names: Wilberforce, Bert, author.
Title: The story of immigration and migration / Bert Wilberforce.
Description: Buffalo, New York : Cavendish Square Publishing, [2024] |
Series: Inside guide: early American history | Includes index.
Identifiers: LCCN 2022053578 (print) | LCCN 2022053579 (ebook) | ISBN 9781502667724 (library binding) | ISBN 9781502667717 (paperback) | ISBN 9781502667731 (ebook)
Subjects: LCSH: Emigration and immigration–History–Juvenile literature. | Migration, Internal–United States–History–Juvenile literature. | United States–Territorial expansion–Juvenile literature. | United States–History–Juvenile literature.
Classification: LCC JV6021 .W56 2024 (print) | LCC JV6021 (ebook) | DDC 304.8/0973–dc23/eng/20221220
LC record available at https://lccn.loc.gov/2022053578
LC ebook record available at https://lccn.loc.gov/2022053579

Editor: Therese Shea
Designer: Deanna Paternostro

The photographs in this book are used by permission and through the courtesy of: Cover, pp. 18, 26 Everett Collection/Shutterstock.com; p. 4 Prostock-studio/Shutterstock.com; p. 6 Cahokia Aerial HRoe 2015/Wikimedia Commons; p. 7 Robert Walter Weir - Embarkation of the Pilgrims - Google Art Project/Wikimedia Commons; p. 8 Indenturecertificate/Wikimedia Commons; p. 9 The Leading Facts of American History (1910) - The First Negro Slaves Brought to Virginia/Wikimedia Commons; p. 10 The British governments in Nth. America - laid down agreeable to the proclamation of Octr. 7, 1763 (NYPL b14968642-435005)/Wikimedia Commons; p. 12 Louisiana Purchase/Wikimedia Commons; p. 13 Lockport bartlett color crop/Wikimedia Commons; p. 14 Nebel Mexican War 12 Scott in Mexico City/Wikimedia Commons; p. 15 An Irish Peasant Family Discovering the Blight of their Store by Daniel MacDonald/Wikimedia Commons; p. 16 Emanuel Leutze - Westward the Course of Empire Takes Its Way - Smithsonian/Wikimedia Commons; p. 19 Oregontrail 1907/Wikimedia Commons; p. 20 SanFranciscoharbor1851c sharp/Wikimedia Commons; p. 21 Winnebago wigwam/Wikimedia Commons; p. 22 Contrabands at Headquarters of General Lafayette by Mathew Brady/Wikimedia Commons; pp. 24–25 Courtesy of the Library of Congress; p. 29 (left) AndriiKoval/Shutterstock.com; p. 29 (right) DnHolm/iStock Photo.

CPSIA compliance information: Batch #CSCSQ24: For further information contact Cavendish Square Publishing LLC at 1-877-980-4450.

Printed in the United States of America

CONTENTS

Immigration and migration shaped the United States. Yet, immigration is an issue of much debate in the country today.

THE EARLIEST IMMIGRANTS

Chapter One

From the first days of settlement in North America, immigration and migration influenced the course of history in the United States. Migration is the movement of people from one place to another, often for work or better living conditions. Immigration is the migration of people into a new country to settle there permanently. The label "immigrant" is often used to describe people who have left their native country. Once they are settled, they may migrate in search of work or a better life.

Native American Migration

The first immigrants to the area that is now the United States were not Europeans. Long before Europeans traveled to the "New World," the first Americans came to North America. Perhaps as long ago as 30,000 years ago, they migrated from Asia to the Americas over a narrow stretch of land that existed at the time called the Bering Land Bridge. These Native

> **Fast Fact**
>
> More than 10,000 years ago, Earth experienced colder climates. More seawater was frozen at the poles, which meant sea levels were lower. That made the route called the Bering Land Bridge possible.

This is an artist's illustration of a Native American city called Cahokia that existed before Europeans arrived in North America. Located near today's St. Louis, Missouri, it was occupied from around 800 to 1400 CE.

peoples gradually moved to different areas and developed different cultures and languages. By the time European explorers arrived in the late 1400s, as many as 18 million Native Americans lived in North America.

Early Immigrations

After the initial European explorations of the New World, Europeans began settling along the eastern coast of North America. The first settlements were little more than military bases. In 1565, Spain founded St. Augustine in today's Florida. It became the first continually inhabited European colony in North America.

Fast Fact

Many early colonists in Jamestown and Plymouth died because they did not have enough supplies or shelter. Others survived thanks to the aid of Native Americans.

This 1857 painting, *The Embarkation of the Pilgrims*, shows the Pilgrims aboard their ship, the *Mayflower*. Some Pilgrims were immigrating to find religious freedom in a new home.

Soon after St. Augustine, other settlements took root along the northeastern coast. Established in 1607, the Jamestown settlement became the foundation for the Virginia colony. Most of the settlers seeking fortune found hardship instead. In 1620, a group later called Pilgrims—including some seeking religious freedom—arrived to found Plymouth in today's Massachusetts. These settlements

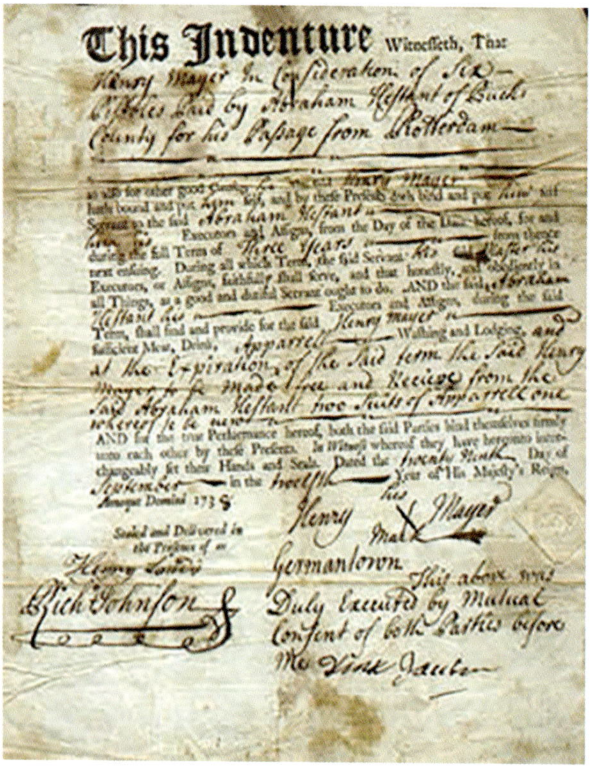
This Indenture Witnesseth, That Henry Mayer in Consideration of Six Pistoles Paid by Abraham Hestant of Bucks County for his Passage from Rotterdam

This indentured servant contract bound a man named Henry Mayer to another man, Abraham Hestant, in Pennsylvania in 1738.

were just the first of many that eventually flourished despite the initial difficulties presented by life in North America.

Many European immigrants made the difficult journey to North America for the promise of farmland. A great number were indentured servants. These were people who, in exchange for passage to the colonies, worked for a number of years for the person who paid for their journey. At the end of that time, some were granted plots of land for their own use. The indentured-servant system often determined where immigrant families settled.

Wealthy immigrants established large farms, sometimes called plantations. Much land in the southern British colonies was used for cotton and tobacco. Wealthy landowners came knowing they could make use of the cheap labor provided by indentured servants and enslaved peoples.

Fast Fact

William Penn came to North America in 1682 to create a colony in which people of all religions (or no religion) could live without persecution. His colony was called Pennsylvania.

THE SLAVE TRADE

You may think of immigration as a **voluntary** act, but many people arrived in the Americas unwillingly. The slave trade transported many Africans to the British colonies of North America beginning in 1619. They were forced to leave their homeland and their freedom. At first, many were treated like indentured servants, but attitudes and laws changed. Soon, enslaved Africans were made to do backbreaking labor for no money and held no rights at all. They were beaten and whipped. Many died. Children born to enslaved mothers became enslaved. Families were broken apart as enslaved family members were sold off. Many Black Americans today are **descendants** of enslaved peoples.

This is an 18th-century illustration of the first enslaved people arriving in Virginia in 1619.

The British Proclamation of 1763 was meant to stop British colonists from settling west of the Appalachian Mountains. The border set by this proclamation is bolded on this map.

A GROWING NATION

Chapter Two

The 13 British colonies of North America started a revolution in 1775, fighting for their independence. Great Britain and the newly formed United States signed the Treaty of Paris in 1783, ending the war. The treaty set the Mississippi River as the western U.S. border. The new government passed laws to encourage citizens to settle in western lands—lands that had belonged to Native Americans. The frontier continuously edged westward.

In 1803, the United States purchased the Louisiana Territory from France, doubling the size of the country. The United States gained control of the Mississippi River and the port city of New Orleans. River settlements—such as St. Louis in Missouri and Memphis in Tennessee—grew as U.S. citizens migrated west.

Fast Fact

The Land **Ordinance** of 1787, or Northwest Ordinance, created a government for the Northwest Territory, which became the states of Illinois, Indiana, Michigan, Ohio, Wisconsin, and part of Minnesota.

A Changing World

Major wars between countries in Europe ended around 1815. Soldiers returning home discovered things were changing. The **Industrial Revolution**

Many states or parts of states were created out of the Louisiana Territory, highlighted here.

made traditional agricultural practices less important in many places. As a result, many soldiers returning from war felt they needed to move, and the United States seemed a hopeful place.

Many immigrants to the United States chose to stay in eastern cities. They often grouped together in neighborhoods, some of which survive to this day. Others migrated to the Midwest. The promise of plentiful inexpensive farmland was a draw for poor European farmers.

One of the most famous early routes inland was human-made. Completed in 1825, the Erie Canal allowed people and goods to travel more quickly and cheaply

Fast Fact

From 1820 to 1860, more than 5 million immigrants came to the United States.

The Erie Canal was an engineering marvel for its time. It linked water routes from the Great Lakes to the Atlantic Ocean.

than ever before. The waterway connected the once-distant locations of Buffalo, New York, and New York City. Cities along the canal grew quickly.

Manifest Destiny

By the 1840s, the idea of Manifest Destiny had become a popular American ideal. Many Americans believed it was the country's destiny to stretch across North America from the Atlantic Ocean to the Pacific. More land meant more resources and more money.

The U.S. government used the idea of Manifest Destiny to justify political and military actions. In 1845, the United States **annexed** the Republic of Texas, which wanted to become a U.S. state. This heightened hostilities between the United States and Mexico, which also claimed Texas. After the U.S. victory in the Mexican-American War in 1848, a treaty gave the United States not only Texas but also the area that is now California, Nevada, Utah, New Mexico, most of Arizona and Colorado, and parts of Oklahoma, Kansas, and Wyoming.

Fast Fact

Americans viewed General Zachary Taylor as a hero after the Mexican-American War. He became president in 1849.

In 1854, the United States paid Mexico $10 million for land that became part of Arizona and New Mexico. This was the Gadsden Purchase. Manifest Destiny had become a reality.

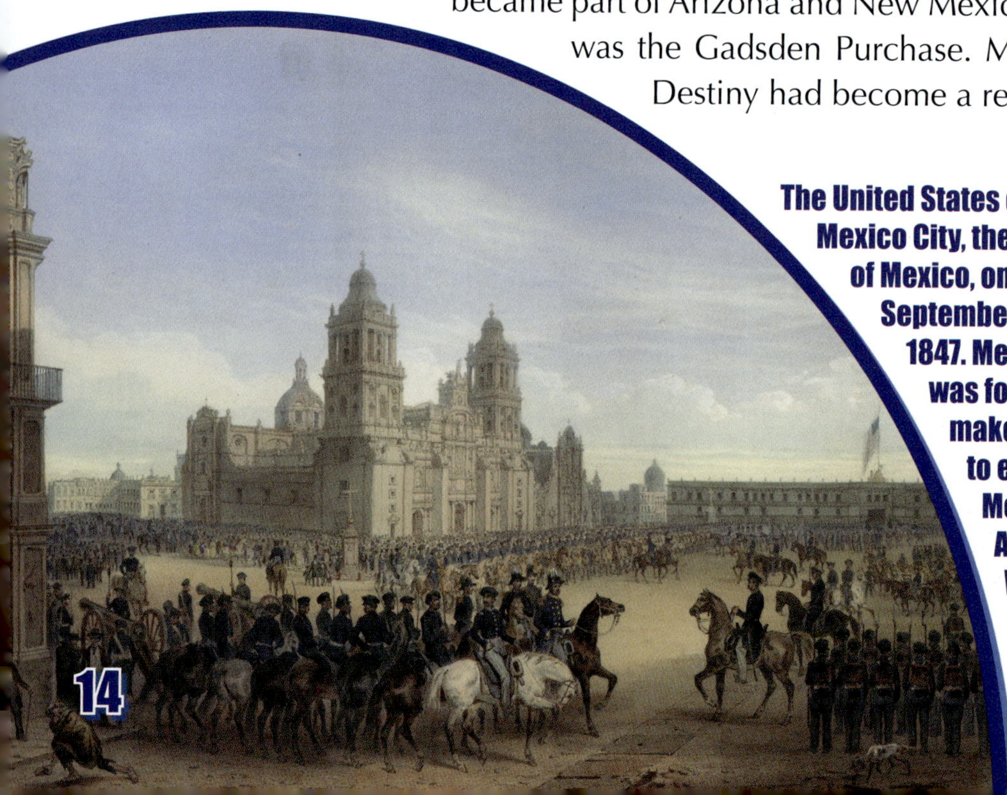

The United States occupied Mexico City, the capital of Mexico, on September 14, 1847. Mexico was forced to make a treaty to end the Mexican-American War.

THE IRISH POTATO FAMINE

From 1845 to 1849, disease caused by a mold began killing Ireland's potatoes, one of the nation's main food sources. More than 1 million people died of starvation or disease during what was called the Irish Potato Famine or Great Famine. That was about one-eighth of the entire population. About 2 million more left Ireland, 1 million of whom immigrated to the United States. Most lived in very poor conditions in eastern cities where it was hard to find jobs. They were often treated poorly. In time, however, Irish immigrants and their descendants became an important part of the industrial growth of the United States.

At the time of the Irish Potato Famine, Great Britain ruled Ireland. The British provided little aid to ease the suffering of the Irish.

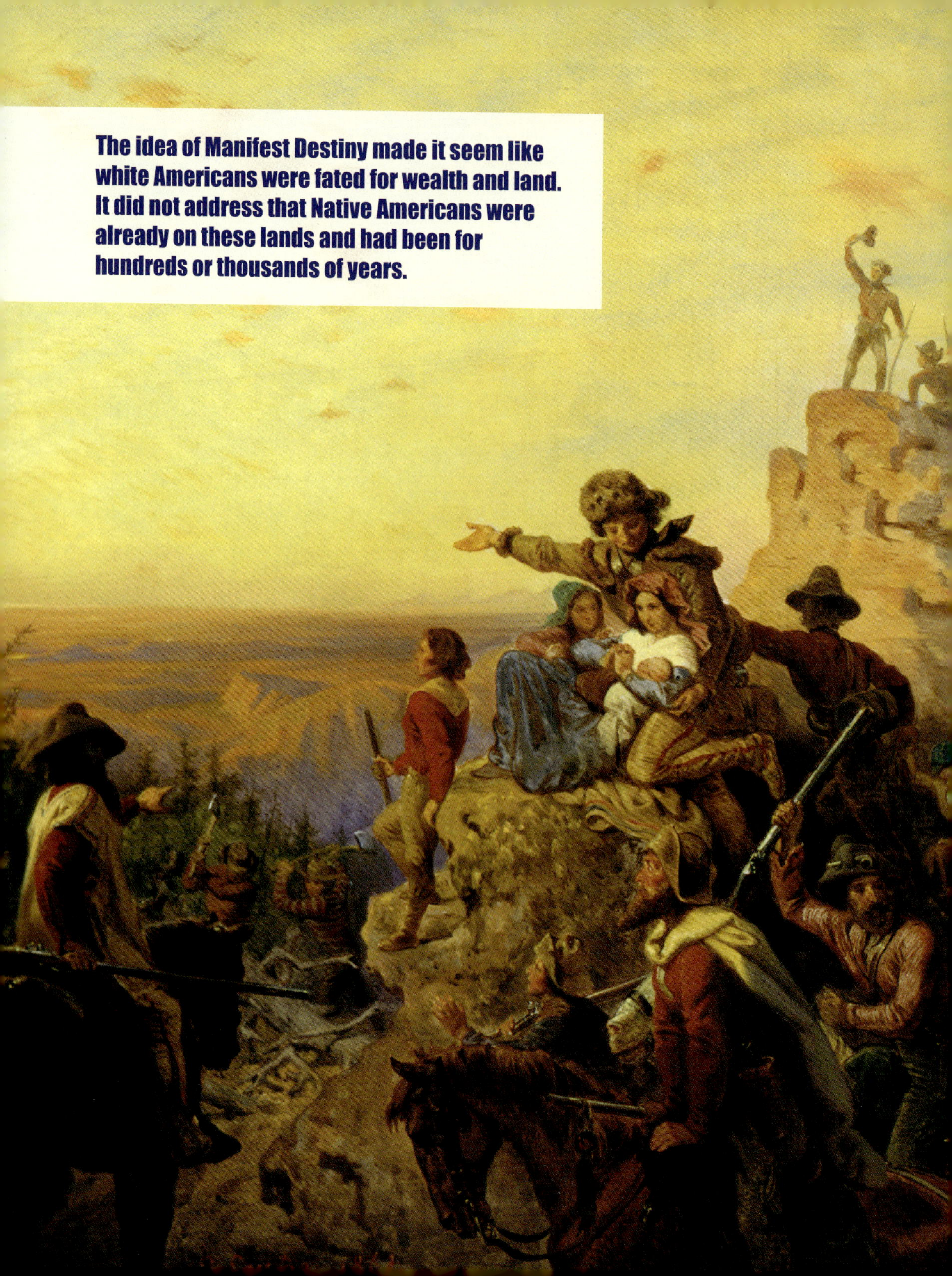

The idea of Manifest Destiny made it seem like white Americans were fated for wealth and land. It did not address that Native Americans were already on these lands and had been for hundreds or thousands of years.

Chapter Three

WESTWARD MOVEMENTS

The Indian Removal Act of 1830 led to about 100,000 Native peoples leaving the eastern United States. In the fall of 1838, the U.S. government began the forced removal of about 15,000 Cherokee from the Southeast. About 4,000 people died of disease, exposure to harsh weather, and starvation on the journey west. Their route and journey became known as the Trail of Tears.

Other Native peoples were also forced from their lands as white settlers moved in. Many were made to live on certain lands called reservations. Some, such as the Ho-Chunk, had to relocate more than once, farther and farther west.

Fast Fact

Many Native American peoples were relocated to Oklahoma, then called Indian Country and later, Indian Territory. In 1889, the U.S. government opened the land to white settlers, causing a "land rush."

Famous Trails

By 1840, about 7 million Americans lived west of the Appalachian Mountains, but even while the West was opening to settlers, traveling there could be difficult and dangerous. Many died from disease and exposure to bad weather. Gradually, people created routes and maps that others could follow. Many paths had been created by Native Americans originally.

From the 1840s to the 1860s, perhaps more than 300,000 pioneers used the Oregon Trail to travel to the Pacific Northwest. The California Trail split off the Oregon Trail in Idaho and headed south to California. The Mormon Trail took travelers, mostly members of the Church of Jesus Christ of Latter-day Saints (often called Mormons), to today's Salt Lake City, Utah. The Santa Fe Trail started in Independence, Missouri, and ended in today's Santa Fe, New Mexico.

Many people migrating west in the 1800s packed their possessions in wagons. This was a slow way to travel.

Fast Fact

The transcontinental railroad cut travel times across the country from months by wagon to just days by train.

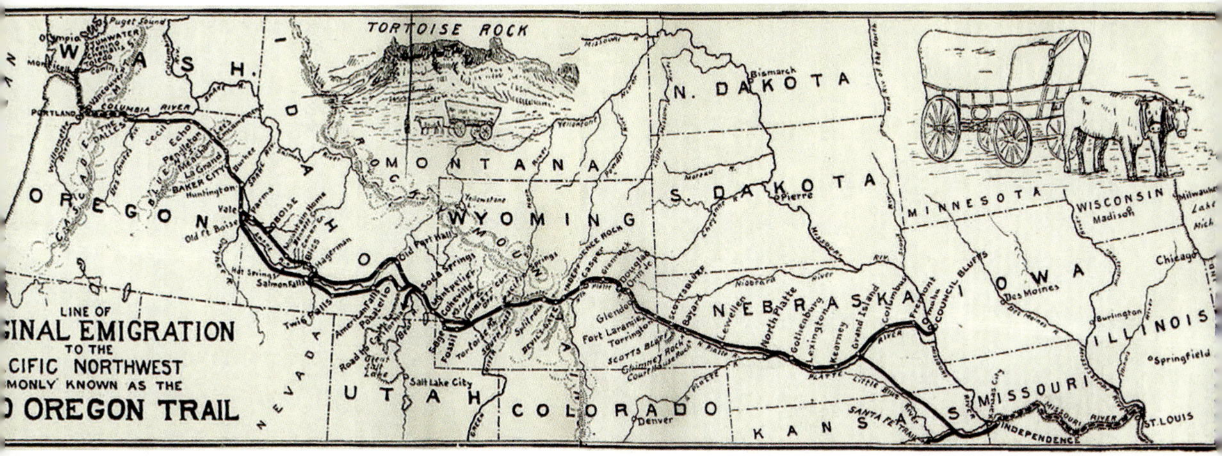

The Oregon Trail was a main migration route west in the mid-1800s. It started in Independence, Missouri, and ended near today's Portland, Oregon.

Later, railways helped Americans migrate. At first, only eastern cities were connected by railroad. In 1854, a railroad was completed that linked the Mississippi River to the Atlantic Ocean. In 1869, the first transcontinental railroad, connecting the East and the West, was finished. Towns grew up along the rail lines. Goods and people could travel more quickly and inexpensively by train. The stream of migration to the West became a river.

The California Gold Rush

While some Americans sought land westward, others were in search of wealth. After gold was discovered in California in 1848, people from around the world rushed to the area in hopes of becoming rich. Some people from the eastern United States traveled by land. Others

Fast Fact

Gold was not the only precious metal that attracted wealth seekers. The discovery of silver in 1859 drew miners to the deposit called the Comstock Lode in today's Nevada.

traveled around South America by ship. Both routes were dangerous and took many months.

Miners from Mexico and South America traveled to California. Chinese miners arrived from Asia by boat. Most forty-niners, as the gold seekers were called, didn't become rich. However, many settled in California permanently. Between 1848 and 1852, California's population swelled from about 15,000 to nearly 225,000 people.

In 1848, San Francisco, California, had about 1,000 inhabitants. By 1850, when this photo was taken, the population was about 25,000.

A COMING CONFLICT

The rapid expansion of the United States contributed to the outbreak of the American Civil War in 1861. As new states were added to the Union, there was much conflict about which states would allow slavery and which would not. Lawmakers made many compromises in the years leading up to the war. No compromise ever settled the issue. The divide between the states over slavery grew wider and more heated. The Southern states finally seceded, or withdrew, from the United States in 1861 after the election of Abraham Lincoln, believing that the president would abolish slavery and cripple the South's economy.

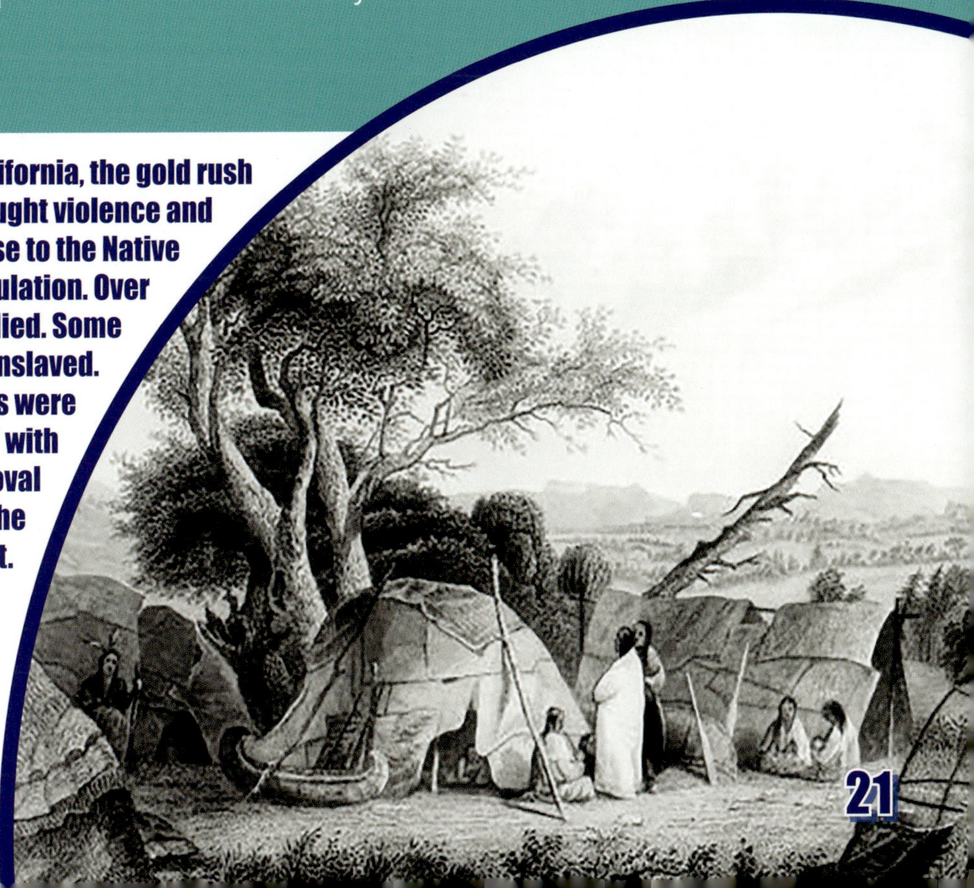

In California, the gold rush brought violence and disease to the Native population. Over 100,000 died. Some were enslaved. Others were murdered with the approval of the government.

In 1865, the American Civil War ended. Much of the South had been destroyed. Slavery was abolished, which meant the Southern economy could no longer rely on agriculture driven by enslaved labor.

AFTER THE CIVIL WAR

Chapter Four

After the Civil War, many people in the South, including Black Americans who had been enslaved, migrated to find work. Some took advantage of the Homestead Act of 1862, which gave lands on the Great Plains to settlers who worked on and improved the land for at least five years. While many white Southerners migrated north, about 10,000 left the country, most immigrating to Brazil where slavery was still legal.

Increasing Immigration

In the 1880s, the number of immigrants entering the United States increased dramatically. The introduction of steam-powered ships made the trip across the Atlantic faster and less expensive. More immigrants came from southern and eastern Europe. The number of immigrants from Asia and the Middle East increased too. Many settled in urban centers across the country where they contributed greatly to the growth of industries and businesses.

Fast Fact

Between 1810 and 1850, an estimated 100,000 enslaved people used **Underground Railroad** routes to the north to find their freedom from slavery.

This photograph from around 1900 shows a street in New York City's Little Italy. The area's nickname comes from the number of Italian immigrants who settled there.

In the late 1800s and early 1900s, numerous anti-Jewish riots—called pogroms—swept across Russia and Poland. About 2 million Jewish people fled the violence and came to the United States by 1914.

The majority of immigrants ended up living in crowded urban areas. Jobs were scarce, and many people remained in poverty. However, immigrants helped build railroads, power lines, gas lines, roads, bridges, and tunnels across the country. Thanks in part to millions of immigrants, the United States became a leading producer of steel, coal, oil, cars, electrical equipment, and other modern necessities.

Changing Laws and Attitudes

Not everyone was warmly welcomed into the United States. People with customs and languages unfamiliar to Americans were sometimes

In 1891, a law barred some people from immigrating to the United States, including those with certain diseases and criminal records. Ellis Island was an immigration station where immigrants were examined, tested, and approved or denied.

Fast Fact

Between 1880 and 1930, about 28 million people immigrated to the United States. Many passed through Ellis Island in New York Harbor. Today, the island is home to an immigration museum.

viewed negatively. The Immigration Act of 1924 limited the number of immigrants through a **quota** system dependent on people's national origin. It completely excluded immigrants from Asia. The larger the population in the United States, the larger the quota. This was an advantage for western Europeans.

In 1965, the Immigration and Nationality Act changed immigration law again. It ended the **discriminatory** quotas. It **prioritized** "highly skilled" immigrants, family members of Americans, and **refugees**. It left out those

STILL AN ESSENTIAL ISSUE

Some fears Americans today have about immigration are similar to the worries of a century ago, such as immigrants taking jobs away from Americans. Others fear people from certain regions of the world, particularly those places that experience **terrorism**. These fears are largely unfounded. Another issue is unauthorized, sometimes called undocumented, immigration. People in poverty in places such as Central and South America have long sought employment in the United States, but the Immigration and Nationality Act of 1965 did not provide for immigration for these people, who often work in sectors that need workers, such as agriculture and construction. It placed a cap on immigrants from the Americas for the first time.

who did not fit in these categories. The immigration laws of today are still based on this act with some changes. For example, the 1990 Immigration Act increased the number of overall immigrants as well as sought to increase diversity by accepting immigrants from lesser represented countries. The United States of today, like the early United States, is still a nation shaped by immigrants.

Fast Fact

In 1882, Congress passed the Chinese Exclusion Act to stop the flow of Chinese immigrants. In 2012, Congress officially regretted the act.

A TIMELINE OF AMERICAN IMMIGRATION AND MIGRATION

1565 Spain founds the St. Augustine settlement.

1607 The Jamestown settlement is founded.

1783 The Treaty of Paris recognizes the United States and establishes borders.

1803 The United States purchases the Louisiana Territory from France.

1825 The Erie Canal is completed.

1834 The U.S. government sets aside "Indian Territory" for Native Americans.

1838 The forced removal of Cherokees—the Trail of Tears—begins.

1845 The United States annexes the Republic of Texas.
The Irish Potato Famine begins.

1848 Gold is discovered in California.

1862 President Abraham Lincoln signs the Homestead Act.

1865 The American Civil War ends, and slavery is abolished.

1869 The transcontinental railroad is completed.

1892 Ellis Island opens as an immigration station.

1889 The Oklahoma (formerly Indian Territory) "land rush" begins.

1924 The Immigration Act establishes an immigration quota system.

1965 The Immigration and Nationality Act ends the immigration quota system.

THINK ABOUT IT!

1. What effect do you think the relocation of Native Americans had on their cultures?
2. How does the economy tie in to immigration and migration?
3. Why do you think some Americans feared (and still fear) groups of immigrants who have different customs and languages?
4. Should unauthorized immigrants be allowed jobs in the United States? Why or why not?

GLOSSARY

annex: To take over an area and make it part of a larger territory.

debate: A prolonged argument or public discussion.

descendant: Someone related to a person who lived in the past.

discriminatory: Unfairly treating people unequally because of their race, origins, cultures, or beliefs.

Industrial Revolution: An era of social and economic change marked by advances in technology from the late 1700s to the mid-1800s.

ordinance: A law or rule.

persecution: Making a group of people suffer cruel or unfair treatment.

prioritize: To make something the most important thing to accomplish or focus on.

proclamation: A public announcement.

quota: An official limit on the number or amount of people or things that are allowed.

refugee: Someone who is seeking a safe place to live, especially during a time of war.

terrorism: The continuous use of violence and fear to challenge an authority.

transcontinental: Extending across a continent.

Underground Railroad: A system to help enslaved people escape to freedom in the northern United States or Canada.

voluntary: Done by choice and not by force.

FIND OUT MORE

Books

Backhaus, Jaclyn. *A New History of Immigration*. New York, NY: Penguin Workshop, 2022.

Holt, Amy. *Should the United States Have Open Borders?* New York, NY: KidHaven Publishing, 2021.

Krull, Kathleen. *American Immigration: Our History, Our Stories*. New York, NY: Harper, 2020.

Websites

Ellis Island
www.ellisisland.org
Learn more about Ellis Island and its significance in the immigrant experience.

How the United States Immigration System Works
www.americanimmigrationcouncil.org/research/how-united-states-immigration-system-works#
Read how the immigration system functions today.

U.S. Immigration
www.pbs.org/destinationamerica/usim.html
This PBS site has many resources about U.S. immigration, including personal stories.

Publisher's note to educators and parents: Our editors have carefully reviewed these websites to ensure that they are suitable for students. Many websites change frequently, however, and we cannot guarantee that a site's future contents will continue to meet our high standards of quality and educational value. Be advised that students should be closely supervised whenever they access the internet.

INDEX